WHEN YOUR LICENSE IS UNDER ATTACK

WHEN YOUR LICENSE IS UNDER ATTACK

A Survival Guide for Texas Professionals

TONY R. BERTOLINO, ESQ.

Arial & Times New Roman fonts used with permission from
Microsoft.

Published by TCK Publishing
www.TCKPublishing.com

ISBN: 978-1-63161-021-9

To my children,
Tony, Natassia & Tatiana

Contents

Introduction

Although the world is full of suffering,
it is also full of the overcoming of it.

~ HELEN KELLER

You finally did it! You studied long hours and obtained a degree from a competitive graduate or post-graduate program. You then filled out and submitted a paper application or applied online to obtain your license to practice your profession. Next, you sat for and passed a rigorous written examination to test your skills and to further convince the boards of your proficiency. You then received your license, and it became official. All the hard work finally paid off.

Excited about your future, you dove into your career. You excelled. Progress! As you climbed the ranks of your profession, the perks followed. You could easily provide for your family, pay your mortgage, and spend your days doing meaningful work that helped others.

Then one evening, everything changed.

You arrived at home after work, as usual, and casually thumbed through the mail. After discarding promotional materials, catalogs and other unsolicited "junk" mail, you came across an envelope addressed by the boards. It struck you as strange: you hadn't received a letter from the boards since they congratulated you on obtaining your license. Why would they be writing you now?

You broke the seal, unfolded the page and began to read. And then it hit you. The boards have accused you of professional misconduct, assigned an investigator and begun an inquiry into whether you violated a Texas law or Board Rule. The boards are threatening sanctions, suspension and even revocation.

YOUR LICENSE IS NOW UNDER ATTACK!

When your professional license is in jeopardy, you have a serious problem. Your livelihood and career is at stake. But you are not alone. In this short survival guide, we will help you understand how to respond strategically to the threat facing your professional credentials. We will also ease your mind about the process and explain the steps you should take to defend yourself the moment you receive a dreaded complaint letter or notice in the mail.

In the following pages, we will explain:

- How to respond strategically to a threat to your license,
- How to minimize disruption to your career or business,
- Steps to maximize your compliance and thus your likelihood of preserving your license and your professional status, and
- Tips for handling "fallout" from your current situation, such as self-doubt, problems at home or with business partners, and uncertainty about planning your next steps.

Section One covers triage – the steps you need to take *now* (within the next week or two) to prepare to advocate strategically for yourself, your license, and your career.

In Section Two, we address the most practical and frequently-asked questions that arise when Texas professionals face license challenges.

QUESTION: I'm a (nurse/physician/real estate broker/other professional). Can this guide really help me in my profession?

Yes! The guide itself provides straightforward and practical advice that applies to any situation in which a professional license is in jeopardy.

In the appendices at the end of this book, we also include profession-specific information to give you a better idea of what to expect in your particular situation. The appendices offer information for Texas nurses (including RNs, LVNs, and Advanced Nurse Practitioners[1]), physicians[2], pharmacists[3], dentists[4], and real estate agents and brokers[5].

In the relevant appendix, you can learn more about the paperwork, deadlines, relevant organizations, and online resources available to help you navigate a license challenge in Texas.

A threat to your hard work and livelihood is tough to face. But are tougher. Here is how to tackle the problem head-on.

---

[1] http://www.bertolinolaw.com/medical-license-defense-lawyers/nurse-license-defense-attorney-tx

[2] http://www.bertolinolaw.com/medical-license-defense-lawyers/physician-license-defense-attorney-tx

[3] http://www.bertolinolaw.com/medical-license-defense-lawyers/pharmacist-license-defense-lawyer-tx

[4] http://www.bertolinolaw.com/medical-license-defense-lawyers/dental-license-defense-lawsuit-tx

[5] http://www.bertolinolaw.com/professional-license-defense-attorneys/real-estate-license-defense-lawyer-tx

SECTION ONE:

Triaging and Effectively Addressing Your Urgency

Develop success from failures.
Discouragement and failure are two
of the surest steppingstones to success.

~ DALE CARNEGIE

Medical professionals know that the first step to providing care in any emergency situation is triage: identifying the most urgent issues and handling them first. In fact, professionals in every field "triage" their most urgent and pressing matters, even if they don't use this term.

When you realize your professional license may be in jeopardy, it may feel like the world is crashing down. What is most urgent? Where should you put your efforts first to ensure you save – or fix – as many things as possible?

Here, we talk about the actions you need to take within the first week or two in order to prepare yourself to advocate strategically for your license and your career.

Picking up this book is a good start. Once you have read what's here, it's time to work the following to-do list:

LEARN ABOUT THE PROCESS

It is very easy to fear a process that is a mystery to you; it is harder to be afraid when you know what to expect. Start by learning how cases against licenses in your field are carried out, and how they are defended.

For example, the Texas Medical Board starts by examining complaints to determine whether the complaint is against someone's TMB licenses, and whether the complained-of act falls under the Medical Practice Act. Other licensing boards handle the process similarly.

Make a list of the steps to come, along with any relevant deadlines. (See the appendices at the end of the book to get an overview of what to expect in your situation.)

CHOOSE YOUR ATTORNEY WISELY

Your lawyer is your partner and best friend in the fight to protect your license and your livelihood. Important questions to ask prospective attorneys during your initial consultation include:

- How many administrative law cases like mine have you handled?
- What were the results of those cases?
- What can I expect in the days and weeks to come? Are there any steps I should take right now?
- How do I contact you or your staff if I have additional questions, or if something comes up?
- What sort of estimated fees or costs can I expect to pay?
- Are you located near Austin? If not, can you still handle the logistics and travel needed to save my license?

It's vital to choose a lawyer with whom you feel comfortable discussing your case – and it's just as vital not to try to "go it alone."

IDENTIFY AND ADDRESS SHORT-TERM DEADLINES

Make sure you know about any upcoming deadlines. List them in your calendar immediately, and set reminders so you do not miss them. For instance, if you have received a letter threatening an investigation or *Notice of Setting* for a hearing, double-check for dates or actions you need to take.

When you talk to your attorney, discuss any pressing deadlines as well. Your lawyer's knowledge of the process will help you plan, so you can be prepared when essential appointments and deadlines arise.

GATHER ALL RELEVANT INFORMATION

In a courtroom or other formal setting, there are specific rules about the sort of information you must preserve and the ways to keep it. When your professional license is at stake, similar rules should guide your thinking. Be sure to gather information that relates to the issue at hand, whether those are complaint/notice letters, medical or pharmacy records, copies of contracts or property listings, emails, photographs, or other items. Also, make a note-log of everything you remember about the situation or incident. Your notes can help guide you and your lawyer as you seek to reconstruct what happened.

MINIMIZE HARM TO YOUR PATIENTS/ CLIENTS/PARTNERS/SUPERVISORS

When your license is being challenged, you may be temporarily prevented from performing certain duties integral to your work. Depending on the situation, your employer or business may come under fire in the media. Take steps to minimize harm to your patients, clients, partner(s), or supervisor by delegating tasks where you can and rearranging your workload so that you can continue to be of service wherever possible. Also, resist the urge to speak to the media. Instead, consult your lawyer for advice on how to address any negative publicity.

WHAT NOT TO DO

It's important to take steps to prepare for a successful outcome. It's just as important to avoid doing things that will undermine your chances. Here's what **NOT** to do when you're facing a license challenge:

- **Contacting your respective Board, Agency or Commission.** Upon your receipt of the notice or complaint letter indicating that you have allegedly violated a board rule or law, you must resist the temptation to call or write to the boards directly. Generally, the boards exist to protect the public by ensuring that standards of practice are met and that professionals are competent in their respective practices. The boards do not represent the best interest of the licensed professional. With that said, do not directly contact the board, agency or commission without first consulting with an attorney.

- **Panic.** Statistically, the Texas Medical Board alone receives over 7,000 complaints a year, many of which end in license scrutiny. Other professional boards or agencies have similar case workloads. The process can be tough, but it follows known rules and systems. In short, don't fear or panic about the process. Experienced help is available.

- **Procrastinate.** Waiting, dawdling, or doing nothing at all may result in your missing an essential deadline, losing key evidence in your favor, or worse. Start taking steps *today* to build a proactive defense. I cannot tell you how many times I have consulted with a potential new client who has waited until the very last day to respond to a complaint or notice. Such actions could compromise the strength of your case and your attorney's ability to adequately prepare. Do yourself a huge favor. Do not procrastinate.

- **Blame Others.** No matter who was ultimately at fault, the challenge you face is to your license, and it's on you to defend it. Save your energy for building a case for *your* license and livelihood. In short, resist the urge to blame a colleague, the client, the patient, the facility, the buyer, the seller, etc.

- **Talk to the Media.** A journalist's job is to tell a story that grabs attention – even when that means leaving out important parts of the story or casting you or others in an unappealing light. Avoid harming your case; present the media with your silence.

- **Try to Go it Alone.** A defense of a professional license is more likely to succeed when you have an ally who understands Texas licensing law and the processes involved. You can be assured that the boards, agency and commissions all have capable and knowledgeable Staff Attorneys on their side.

So, do not try to represent yourself and go "toe-to-toe" against a Staff Attorney.   You will lose. Instead, choose a knowledgeable license defense lawyer who has a solid winning record.

SECTION TWO:

Frequently Asked Questions

I learned that courage was not the absence of fear, but the triumph over it.

The brave man is not he who does not feel afraid, but he who conquers that fear.

~ NELSON MANDELA

When your professional license is under fire, questions are normal. In this section, we gather some of the most commonly-asked questions professionals have when facing a license challenge.

Question: How do I regain control of my to-do list?

Getting organized and staying productive in the face of a license challenge is tough – and essential. For staying on top of your commitments in a trying time, we like David Allen's Getting Things Done (GTD) method.

GTD is a method for organizing your to-dos, priorities, and schedule so that you can manage what's ahead. It can be as complicated or as simple as you need, but here are the basics.

Capture

The first step to getting things done is to know what needs doing. Use the simplest, most accessible method for you to jot down all your to-dos, your ideas, your recurring tasks, and everything else.

Clarify

Big overwhelming tasks, like "handle license problem," don't get done; specific, actionable steps do. This is where you start to figure out what needs to be done and when.

When the steps are clear, you can easily handle things you can handle right away and delegate what you can't. (We talk more about effective delegation below).

Organize

Once you have a list of actionable items, sort them by category and priority. If an item has a due date, write that in as well. Think of this step as "quality time" with your to-do list, inbox, or calendar. You are not *doing* any of the tasks now; you are just making sure everything is where it needs to be.

If you have trouble organizing the list, try these methods:

- **"Big task, little tasks":** First, write down each "big task" you are trying to accomplish, like "beat license challenge" or "get someone else to take over my patients." These are your big categories. Under each one, list the tasks that need to be done to achieve the goal in order of priority. For instance, your first step in "beat license challenge" might be "call an attorney." Your first step in "get someone to take over my files" might be "go talk to my business partner/supervisor."

- **Urgent and/or important:** To help you prioritize tasks, mark them as follows. If the task is both urgent (time-sensitive) *and* important (big cost for not doing it), mark it "UI." If it is urgent but not important (for instance, taking out the trash), mark it "U." If it is important but not urgent (for instance, helping your child with homework), mark it "I." If it is neither urgent nor important, mark it "X." Tasks marked "UI" go near the top of the list. Tasks marked "X" can often be left off the list completely.

Reflect

Once your list is in shape, look it over. What's your next step? If you have put in the time to clarify, picking something you can do right away should be simple. Spend time every day reviewing the list to make sure you're making progress on key tasks, adjusting your priorities when needed, and changing the system so that it works for you.

Engage

Now, it's time to get to work. Pick an item from your list and do it. Now that your tasks are organized by priority and category, you can easily choose things that will give you the biggest "bang for your buck" with the time and energy you should devote to them *right now*.

QUESTION: How do I delegate to others at work in a professional, effective, and efficient way?

Effective delegating is an important skill to learn. Here's how to practice it:

Choose the right person for the task

Make your first choice for every task the person who is best equipped to handle it. Have a second choice in mind as well. Delegating thoughtfully helps ensure that your patients or clients receive the quality care and service they need.

Give them all the information

Ensure the person who agrees to take on the task has the information they need to do it. This may mean providing patient or client names, handing over charts or files, and making written notes to describe where you were in the process of assisting a particular patient or client when you were interrupted, and what is left to complete.

Let go…

Resist the urge to micromanage once you have handed off the task and the necessary information. The purpose of delegating is to reduce your stress load while ensuring vital tasks are taken care of – and your stress load does not go down if you "hover" after delegating a task.

…but check in periodically

Be available to answer questions or offer advice if it is needed, within the scope of the duties you are currently allowed to perform. If you are prevented from doing this, ask someone with the necessary credentials to step in for you to provide advice or guidance where it's needed.

Focus on what you *can* do

If you are forced to delegate due to a license challenge, you may feel somewhat "adrift" as parts of your job suddenly become off-limits.

Instead, focus your energy on the tasks you can still do, including preparing to defend your license vigorously.

QUESTION: I'm falling apart. How can I "keep it together" during this trying time in my life?

The threat of losing your license – and your livelihood – can derail even the most stoic and organized among us.

During periods of high stress, it's vital to practice self-care. Healthy behaviors build a foundation from which you can respond proactively to the challenges to come.

Here's how.

Make room for your feelings

Your feelings are what they are – even when they are unpleasant or conflict with one another. Telling yourself "I can't feel like this right now" or "I'm not going to get angry/sad/etc." may seem to work in the short term, but in the long term it will cause more problems than it solves.

Instead, make space for your feelings in the following ways:

- **Talking about them.** Work with a professional therapist (or your church) or simply speak to a trustworthy friend or family member. Choose someone who is willing to listen and acknowledge that your feelings are real, no matter what they are.

- **Expressing them in other ways.** If you have a hobby or an artistic outlet you enjoy, it can be a profound way to express your feelings. Journaling is powerful as well. For some people, taking out stress on a punching bag or with vigorous exercise can help them regain clarity (and maintain health). And, of course, crying is a valid and useful tool for many people with pent-up frustration, anger, or grief.

We all try, at times, to push away unpleasant emotions. They are "unpleasant" because we do not want to feel them!

Learning to sit with them, however, can help you work through them faster than ignoring them, bottling them up, or pushing them away.

Practice healthy habits – even the little ones

With a new crisis on your plate, sticking to your usual healthy eating, sleeping, and exercise routine might feel difficult or impossible. But having to scale back healthy habits doesn't mean having to abandon them entirely.

Consider:

- **Packing healthy snacks.** You may not have time for a nutritious meal on a day when you are running to and from meetings, or when you should appear for a noon hearing. But you can choose to pack granola, protein bars, fruit, or yogurt, instead of relying on the mercy of vending machines.

- **Taking a short walk.** Even if your schedule forces you to skip the gym, you can likely find time to take a ten- to fifteen-minute walk around the block. This will help clear your head and release physical tension.

- **Taking a short mental break.** Several studies have confirmed the benefit of a 20-minute "power nap." Even if you can't doze off, simply listening to soothing music or taking a few minutes to pay attention to your breathing can help calm you, reduce tension, and clear your mind for what's ahead.

Getting through a stressful situation like a license challenge is a marathon, not a sprint. It's important to keep fueling (and resting) your body and brain at intervals so you can survive the long haul.

Practice taking the long perspective

When our stress hormones build up, relatively small problems can start to look like insurmountable ones. When you start to feel overwhelmed or like the situation is catastrophic, visualize yourself in five or ten years. Where are you? What are you doing? Which of the most important parts of your life are still present, in one form or another?

This simple exercise can help you keep your current challenge in perspective without belittling it or yourself. It can also help you clarify your current goals, so that you stand a better chance of reaching them.

Question: How did this happen?

Learning from a crisis and identifying ways to prevent it in the future are two of the most valuable opportunities we have – if we can seize them.

One way to analyze the problem and find its root causes is by using a "5-Why" analysis. By asking "Why?" five times in a row, we can often drill down to the root cause of a problem – and by addressing that root cause, we can resolve every other problem identified during the process.

Here's how the "5-Why" analysis might work in a hypothetical license challenge scenario. Imagine that a physician is facing a license challenge due to significant errors in charting that led to the physician prescribing a medication to which the patient was known to be severely allergic.

Our hypothetical physician begins by identifying a symptom of the problem:

I failed to note that the patient was severely allergic to this medication, even when the patient told me.

Then, our hypothetical physician asks, "Why?"

I was thinking about some lab tests I had ordered for another patient.

Why?

I was worried that the results would come back inconclusive or untrustworthy.

Why?

Our lab equipment is outdated, and I'm not sure the new staff members have the training they need to operate it correctly.

Why?

We have been trying to use that equipment long enough to "get our money's worth," because we're worried that sending out tests to other labs (like the one at the local hospital) will be expensive and time-consuming.

Why?

Now that I think about it, we don't really know what the process is for sending out our labs. We've just assumed it's a hassle, and we haven't made it a priority to find out whether that's true.

The fifth time through, our hypothetical physician has discovered the root cause of the problem: she and her partners in their medical practice do not know what their options are for improving the quality of lab results. This is a problem that can be addressed.

By addressing it, our physician and her fellow doctors also address the other symptoms identified: they do not have to rely on outdated equipment; they do not need to worry about the training their staff have on running the tests; and they have one less thing to distract them from paying attention to each patient and their needs.

While a "5-Why?" analysis may not fend off a license investigation you are already facing, it can help you prevent yourself and those you work with from making the same mistake twice. It can also demonstrate a proactive good-faith effort to understand and improve the situation. It can also be used as a "mitigating factor" when the boards are considering sanctions against a professional's license.

What happens if the "worst case scenario" occurs?

When faced with any kind of threat, most of us do not want to think about the worst-case scenario. When we do not look at it head-on, however, it lurks in the background, constantly poking at our thoughts – and causing anxiety that can lead to bad decisions.

When we *do* look at it, the process can be surprisingly transformative. Understanding and embracing the worst possible outcome can rebuild your sense of control, suggest effective ways for avoiding the worst, and help you clarify and reach your goals.

Here's how to do it. Start with a piece of paper (or a blank word-processing file). Write at the top: "What is the worst thing that could happen?"

Then, list the possibilities. For most professionals facing license challenges, the first possibility is "I will lose my license and not be able to practice anymore." Possibilities like "I will lose my job here," "I will lose my business," "I will lose my career and have to pay steep fines," and "I will not be able to support my family" may also appear on your list, depending on the circumstances.

For each possibility, imagine yourself in that situation. Picture what you will do then. For instance, if your worst-case scenario is "I will lose my license and career," imagine yourself having already lost it. Your options might include getting a different job in your field, going back to school, or moving into a different field in which similar skills are called for.

The more options you can picture for each "worst case scenario" on your list, the more opportunities you give yourself and the more your sense of control over the situation grows. And if the worst doesn't happen – and, often, it does not (particularly within my law practice when defending a client) – you can feel confident knowing that you have your life under control either way.

**I have a question that's not answered here.
What should I do?**

Although these are some of the most common questions, they are certainly not the only questions asked. If you need more information or answers to your additional questions, talk to an attorney with experience representing professionals and their licenses.

Conclusion

*"In order to succeed, people need a sense
of self-efficacy, to struggle together with
resilience to meet the inevitable obstacles
and inequities of life."*

~ ALBERT BANDURA

Facing a board investigation and license challenge is
not easy. And, while it might be a character-building
experience, very few people would decide to build
their character in this way if they had a choice.

Nevertheless, you are here, and it's time to get to work and
do what you have to do.

You have already taken one important step toward getting
your life back on track and standing up to a license
challenge by reading this book. Now, it's time to put some
of the tips and recommendations in these pages to work.
Triage your situation, prioritize and organize your "to-do"

list, and choose one action you can take *today* that will help you stay in control of your situation and move forward.

There is another important step we recommend you take today.

We recommend you contact our law firm to discuss your options. It's important to explore your options so you can find a lawyer you trust, we are ready to help you understand what you are facing and create a plan of action that will move you toward your most important goals. We have vast experience representing Texas professionals in your situation, from nurses, doctors, and dentists to pharmacists and real estate agents and brokers. We are ready to help.

The reason our law firm exists is to help professionals, like you, keep their licenses when those licenses are under attack by a Texas state agency or board. That's all we do. We are passionate about our mission.

For insight into your case, please visit www.bertolinolaw.com to schedule your initial consultation online, or call our legal team today at **(512) 476-5757**. Our law firm represents licensed professionals in the cities of Austin, Houston, San Antonio, Dallas and throughout the state of Texas.

Get in touch now: we can give you the strategic road map and peace of mind you deserve.

APPENDIX A:

For Nurses (RN, LVN, NP)[6]

Nurses occupy a unique place when it comes to their licenses. Many nurses are employed by the practice or hospital where they work (unlike physicians, who may own the practice or have admitting privileges in a hospital without being employed by that hospital).

While nurses may not practice medicine, they are held to high standards of patient care and may face repercussions if those standards are not met.

Like other professionals, a nurse who faces a disciplinary action by the licensing board, may also face certain consequences. These may include a fine or an encumbrance on the license, such as a suspension. Upon

---

6 http://www.bertolinolaw.com/medical-license-defense-lawyers/nurse-license-defense-attorney-tx

disposition of a case, the results of a disciplinary action are also posted on the website of the Texas Board of Nursing (BON) and published in the *Texas Board of Nursing Bulletin*, which is distributed quarterly. This means that the results of a disciplinary action may follow you for many years, no matter where you go.

An allegation against you by the Texas BON is serious. Here's what to do if you're facing one or you suspect that you soon will face one.

SPEAK TO A LAWYER

A challenge to your license may feel like an attack on the hard work you have put in to earn your credentials and care for your patients. An attorney is your best ally in defending against that attack and protecting your livelihood. And definitely do not contact the Texas Board of Nursing on your own.

Choose your lawyer wisely. Administrative law is a unique area of law, with many rules and procedures that appear nowhere else. An administrative defense proceeding involving a Texas nursing license draws from criminal, civil, and administrative law. Thus, you will want to choose a lawyer with experience representing licensed professionals, including nurses, in Texas.

WATCH OUT FOR DEADLINES

Letters from the Texas BON often include a specific step you must take next, and a date by which you must take that step. Note these deadlines in your personal calendar, phone, or day planner the moment you see them. Then, act quickly to ensure that you handle the issue well before the due date.

Many nurses in Texas end up facing disciplinary consequences simply because they ignored a communication from the BON. Do not take this risk. Stay on top of deadlines, and communicate promptly with your lawyer about them, as well.

PUT YOUR BEST PROFESSIONAL FOOT FORWARD

From the clothing you choose to the way you carry yourself and how you speak, the more professional you can appear, the more likely it is that the BON will take your version of events and your approach to the matter seriously. Focus on projecting an air of respect for the proceedings and examining your arguments and evidence until you know every detail.

KNOW WHAT YOU PLAN TO SAY AHEAD OF TIME

As your lawyer will explain, documentation is one of the strongest tools available to help you protect your license. Items like medical records, notes, and other forms of documentation will provide the backbone of your case. Work with your lawyer to gather and examine the documentation that supports your defense.

As you examine documentation and speak with your lawyer, prepare for what you plan to say at any upcoming hearing or other appearance before the BON. Be willing to admit error where it exists, and talk about the steps you are taking to ensure that a similar mistake never happens again. If speaking about a particular issue or event might incriminate you, speak to your attorney about how to handle it[7] well in advance of any hearing or appearance before the Texas Board of Nursing.

---

[7] http://www.bertolinolaw.com/medical-license-defense-lawyers/nurse-license-defense-attorney-tx

APPENDIX B:

For Physicians[8]

T he Texas Medical Board, also known simply as the "Board" or "TMB", brings license investigations and allegations against physicians in Texas.

Once a disciplinary action by the TMB is finalized, it is posted both to the National Practitioner Data Bank (NPDB) and to the TMB's own website. As a result, your professional reputation nationwide may be affected by how you respond to a license challenge or disciplinary action.

Potential penalties include completing additional continuing medical education (CMEs) courses, severe

---

8 http://www.bertolinolaw.com/medical-license-defense-lawyers/physician-license-defense-attorney-tx

fines, encumbrances on your license, including potential suspension or even revocation of your license.

Meanwhile, the legal proceedings draw from both civil and criminal law practices, as well as rules specific to administrative law. Choosing an attorney who is vastly experienced in administrative defense, and who understands how to protect physicians specifically, is a must.

In addition to choosing an attorney with experience and a track record of success, the following steps can also help you protect your license and your livelihood:

USE YOUR BEST PROFESSIONAL BEHAVIOR

Projecting an air of professionalism communicates that you respect the gravity of the situation and the authority of the TMB. This, in turn, can have a significant positive impact on your situation. Regardless of the nature of the allegations you face, focus on projecting full professional decorum at all times.

BE WILLING TO ADMIT WHERE YOU WERE WRONG

Earlier in this guide, we discussed methods you can use to find the root cause of a problem and identify steps to correct it.

Being willing to admit where you have made a mistake, discuss how you used this process to examine what happened, and describe the steps you are taking to ensure no such mistake happens again can help build your case for less damaging disciplinary actions.

DOCUMENT EVERYTHING

Thorough documentation is invaluable when building a case to protect your license. Copies of medical records, your notes, emails, letters, and other documentation will help you establish what happened, what you did, and to what extent any complaint against you is founded.

Work with your lawyer to review and understand every detail of the documentation that supports your case.

RESPOND PROMPTLY WHEN YOU RECEIVE A NOTICE FROM THE TMB

A surprising number of Texas physicians are disciplined each year not because the complaints against them were fully founded, but because they ignored a written notice from the TMB until it was too late to respond. If you ignore a notice, you may find yourself facing disciplinary action by default and lose your day in "court."

Instead, confer with an attorney and respond promptly, and well within any deadline stated in the complaint letter. Be proactive in working with your lawyer to build the strongest defense.

PREPARE TO SPEAK FOR YOURSELF AT THE INFORMAL SETTLEMENT CONFERENCE (ISC)

Your lawyer can help guide you[9] when it comes to deciding what you should say and how you should say it. However, the physicians who fare best in disciplinary hearings (i.e., Informal Settlements) are those who convey confidence, understanding, and clarity when they speak for themselves in front of the TMB. Take the time to understand all the details of the situation and to determine what you most need to say in order to explain your side of the story and refute any challenges from the TMB.

---

[9]   http://www.bertolinolaw.com/medical-license-defense-lawyers/physician-license-defense-attorney-tx

APPENDIX C:

For Pharmacists[10]

Pharmacists, Pharmacies and Pharmacy Technicians in Texas are licensed through the Texas State Board of Pharmacy, which also handles complaints and, when the Board feels it necessary, disciplinary actions.

When a disciplinary action against a pharmacist in Texas is finalized, the results are posted to the Texas State Board of Pharmacy website. The results become publicly available not only within the state of Texas, but nation- and worldwide – and the content of those results can have significant effects on your professional reputation anyplace those results can be viewed.

---

[10] http://www.bertolinolaw.com/medical-license-defense-lawyers/pharmacist-license-defense-lawyer-tx

If you are facing a challenge to your license as a practicing pharmacist, it's vital that you take steps to protect yourself, your license, and your livelihood. Here's how.

CHOOSE AN EXPERIENCED ATTORNEY

If the Pharmacy Board finds that a complaint or allegation against you is warranted, you may face a steep fine, a suspension or other encumbrance on your license, or – in the worst case scenario – the loss of your license.

Administrative law is unlike any other area of law. Professional license challenges are even more complex, as they draw from principles of criminal and civil law as well as administrative law. As a result, your best defense is to work with a lawyer who has successfully represented pharmacists facing license challenges in the past.

RESPOND PROMPTLY TO ANY NOTICES FROM THE PHARMACY BOARD

Every year, one or more pharmacists in Texas are disciplined not because they stood up for their license and lost, but because they ignored a notice from the Pharmacy Board. Avoid losing the fight before it even begins: respond promptly to any notice the Board sends, and well before the applicable deadline. Your lawyer can help you make a strong, timely response.

PRACTICE BEING PROFESSIONAL AND HUMBLE

The attitude and approach the pharmacist takes plays a significant role in the outcome of many license challenges. It pays to treat the proceedings and those involved in them as a serious matter worthy of your best professional respect – and to save your personal view of the matter for private conversations.

Likewise, you can often help your own case by being willing to admit when a mistake was made, and to discuss the steps you have taken to prevent that mistake from ever happening again. It is the purpose of disciplinary hearings to protect the public from incompetent or uncaring pharmacists. By demonstrating your willingness to admit error and to take proactive steps to correct the situation, you demonstrate that you belong among the competent and caring professionals who make up the vast majority of pharmacists in Texas – and that you should be allowed to remain there.

WORK WITH YOUR LAWYER TO GATHER DOCUMENTATION AND MAKE THE BEST CASE FOR YOURSELF.

Expressing a professional, respectful demeanor and being able to admit and correct mistakes can have a significant impact on the outcome of any challenge to your license. In addition, being willing and prepared to speak on your own behalf demonstrates confidence, a proactive approach, and a willingness to work with the Board to ensure that patients in Texas receive proper care. Resist the urge to rely on your attorney to speak for you in all circumstances. Instead, work with your lawyer[11] to gather as much documentation relating to the complaint as you can, to understand every detail of that evidence, and to practice explaining your side of the story and refuting any claims the Board makes against you or your license.

---

[11] http://www.bertolinolaw.com/medical-license-defense-lawyers/pharmacist-license-defense-lawyer-tx

APPENDIX D:

For Dentists[12]

The Texas State Board of Dental Examiners both licenses dental professionals in Texas and handles disciplinary actions against those licensed professionals. Any allegation or complaint filed against you with the Board could jeopardize your career – whether or not it has merit.

Once a disciplinary decision by the Board is made final, it is posted to the Texas State Board of Dental Examiners website. In other words, it becomes available for the public to search from anyplace in the world that has an Internet connection. As a result, it may affect your professional reputation anywhere in the country – or even the world.

---

12 http://www.bertolinolaw.com/medical-license-defense-lawyers/dental-license-defense-lawsuit-tx

It is vital, then, to address any notice from the Board in a prompt and thorough manner. Here is how.

CONTACT AN EXPERIENCED LAWYER

Administrative law differs in complex and detailed ways from other areas of law. Disciplinary proceedings against professional licenses are even more complex. As a "quasi-criminal" area of law, these proceedings draw from Texas administrative law, criminal law, and civil law in order to build the rules by which they are carried out.

Consequently, the lawyer best equipped to help you successfully defend against a license challenge is one who has experience representing dentists and dental professionals in proceedings before the Texas State Board of Dental Examiners.

RESPOND PROMPTLY TO NOTICES FROM THE BOARD

Ignoring a notice from the Board can be tempting, especially if you feel that the complaints against you are unfounded or frivolous. Failing to respond to a notice, however, may result in a disciplinary action being taken against your license by default.

Instead, read each notice thoroughly. Make a note of any action you are required to take and the date by which you must take it. Then, act well in advance of that deadline to notify your lawyer, gather documentation, and prepare to address the issue. In any challenge to a professional license, the most successful dental professionals are those who take a proactive approach to responding to the Board and to building their own defense.

GATHER AND PRESERVE DOCUMENTATION

Documentation is the backbone of a case to protect a professional license. When you can provide the records, notes, letters, and other documentation to back up your recollection of events, you can establish a credible case to protect your license. Work with your attorney to gather documentation, study and understand it thoroughly, and be able to recount the details.

PRACTICE PROFESSIONAL DECORUM

A challenge to your license can spark a host of negative and conflicting feelings. When you appear before the Board, however, your license and your livelihood need you to practice your best professional behavior. Dress in your best business professional attire, project a professional air, and treat the proceedings with respect.

It is particularly helpful to prepare with your attorney[13] to speak on your own behalf before the Board. Focus on how you will discuss the events, admit any errors you made, and explain what steps you have taken to ensure those mistakes do not happen again. When you fully understand

---

[13] http://www.bertolinolaw.com/medical-license-defense-lawyers/dental-license-defense-lawsuit-tx

the details of the situation and can discuss them professionally and thoughtfully, you help to demonstrate that the Board can and should trust you to continue practicing your profession.

APPENDIX E:

For Real Estate Agents/Brokers[14]

Practicing real estate in Texas is a job for which you have long prepared, and earned your license. An allegation brought against you by the Texas Real Estate Commission (TREC) can feel like an attack.

Once any disciplinary action by TREC is finalized, its results become part of the public record – and they are published on the Commission's website, making them available to anyone with an Internet connection. The results of a disciplinary action, then, can affect you long after any fines are paid or periods of suspension are served.

---

[14] http://www.bertolinolaw.com/professional-license-defense-attorneys/real-estate-license-defense-lawyer-tx

Here is how to ensure you meet the challenge and build a strong defense to protect your license, your career, and your livelihood.

START BY CHOOSING AN EXPERIENCED ATTORNEY

Administrative law is unique. While administrative proceedings against real estate licenses in Texas combine elements of criminal, civil, and administrative law, they fully "match" none of these legal areas.

As a result, the best ally in a disciplinary proceeding against your license is a lawyer who has experience defending real estate agents and brokers who have faced license challenges. Choose an attorney who specializes in administrative defense and who can help you navigate this equally specialized area of law.

PAY ATTENTION TO DEADLINES

Every year, real estate agents, brokers, and other professionals in Texas find themselves facing disciplinary action because they ignored or forgot a deadline imposed by TREC. Do not become one of them.

Open all letters and notices from TREC promptly, read them to learn what steps you need to take and by what deadline, and act well in advance of the deadline. Doing so helps ensure that you protect your rights and build a strong defense for your license and livelihood.

BE PROFESSIONAL, YET HUMBLE

Using your best professional dress and behavior in front of TREC is an excellent way to demonstrate respect for the proceedings and to establish yourself as someone who takes the situation seriously. This, in turn, encourages TREC to treat your license with the gravity it deserves.

When you prepare to speak to TREC, focus on a thoughtful, realistic approach that focuses on the issues. If you made a mistake, admit it. Talk about what you learned, and describe the steps you have taken to ensure that a similar mistake never happens again.

WORK CLOSELY WITH YOUR LAWYER.

Your lawyer can help you prepare, understand, and organize both the documentation that supports your case and the things you will say to TREC to defend your position.

Documentation that supports your side of the story is one of the strongest tools at your disposal for defending your real estate license. Make gathering the paperwork your priority, and work closely with your lawyer[15] to examine and understand every detail.

Your lawyer can also help you prepare any statements you plan to make before TREC. It is wise to speak on your own behalf when you can do so, as it demonstrates your

---

[15] http://www.bertolinolaw.com/professional-license-defense-attorneys/real-estate-license-defense-lawyer-tx

willingness to take responsibility for the situation – a trait the Commission tends to prize. If any particular statement or issue might incriminate you, talk it over with your lawyer well before your Commission appearance.

About the Author

Tony R. Bertolino is founder of BERTOLINO LLP, a premier boutique law firm that is on a mission to help Texas professionals defend their licenses.

Tony's passion is finding solutions to his clients' serious personal and professional problems. He also takes pride that out of the many thousands of clients that he and his legal team have defended, they have never lost a license to revocation.

Tony lives and works in downtown Austin, Texas. In addition to being an attorney, writer, speaker, litigator, and foodie, he is also a dad to three beautiful children.

To learn more about Tony and his legal services, please visit www.bertolinolaw.com.

DISCLAIMER

Disclaimer for **"When Your License is Under Attack: A Survival Guide for Texas Professionals"**

You understand that this book is not intended as a substitution for a consultation with an attorney. Downloading, requesting or otherwise viewing this book and the information in it does not create an attorney-client relationship with BERTOLINO LLP or any of its attorneys. To obtain legal advice about your administrative law matter, please engage the services of BERTOLINO LLP or another law firm of your choice. To discuss engaging BERTOLINO LLP to help you with your matter, please contact the firm.

BERTOLINO LLP IS PROVIDING **"WHEN YOUR LICENSE IS UNDER ATTACK: A SURVIVAL GUIDE FOR TEXAS PROFESSIONALS"** (HEREAFTER REFERRED TO AS "BOOK") AND ITS CONTENTS ON AN "AS IS" BASIS AND MAKES NO REPRESENTATIONS OR WARRANTIES OF ANY KIND WITH RESPECT TO THIS BOOK OR ITS CONTENTS. BERTOLINO LLP DISCLAIMS ALL SUCH REPRESENTATIONS AND WARRANTIES, INCLUDING FOR EXAMPLE WARRANTIES OF MERCHANTABILITY AND FITNESS FOR A PARTICULAR PURPOSE. IN ADDITION, BERTOLINO LLP DOES NOT REPRESENT OR WARRANT THAT THE INFORMATION

ACCESSIBLE VIA THIS BOOK IS ACCURATE, COMPLETE OR CURRENT.

The book is provided for information purposes only, and relevant laws frequently change. Except as specifically stated in this book, neither BERTOLINO LLP nor any authors, contributors, or other representatives will be liable for damages arising out of or in connection with the use of this book. This is a comprehensive limitation of liability that applies to all damages of any kind, including (without limitation) compensatory; direct, indirect or consequential damages; loss of data, income or profit; loss of or damage to property, and claims of third parties and punitive damages.

We can help you fight back if
your license is under attack by a
Texas state board or commission.

Call the Bertolino Law Firm at
(512) 476-5757

or learn more at
www.bertolinolaw.com